Walt Farmer
505 Ponderosa Dr.
Jackson (Hole), WY 83001

# -GERMANY-

# Michael Ruetz

# -GERMANY-

*With an Introduction by Joachim Kaiser*

A Bulfinch Press Book · Little, Brown and Company

Boston · Toronto · London

Frontispiece: Avenue of trees in Sieseby on the Schlei, Schleswig-Holstein
The publisher and the photographer thank the German Lufthansa Corporation for their kind assistance.

First English language Edition, 1990
First published in the Federal Republic of Germany by Süddeutscher Verlag
Translated from the German by Deborah Lucas Schneider


Library of Congress Cataloging-in-Publication Data

Ruetz, Michael.
    [Deutschland. English]
    Germany / Michael Ruetz; introduction by Joachim Kaiser. – 1st
U.S. ed.
        p. cm.
    Translation of: Deutschland.
    "A Bulfinch Press book."
    ISBN 0-8212-1795-X
    1. Germany (West) — Description and travel — 1981- — Views.
I. Title.
DD258.35.R8413 1990
943 – dc20
                                                                89-82090
                                                                CIP


Bulfinch Press is an imprint and trademark of Little, Brown and Company (Inc.)
Published simultaneously in Canada by Little, Brown & Company (Canada) Limited

PRINTED IN THE FEDERAL REPUBLIC OF GERMANY

*Dedicated to my friends in the GDR*
M. R.

# Germany: Vision and Reality

## by Joachim Kaiser

### I.

There is a "real" Germany, the Germany of statistics and a booming economy. The "German question" is real, too, with all the risks and perpetual uncertainty associated with it: What territory does the term "Germany" include? And how did this territory come to be defined as one nation and unified as a country? At the time when France, Spain, and England were developing into compact monarchies, we Germans – although "we" had been able to play a strikingly dominant role in the Middle Ages – could achieve no more than a loose confederation of small principalities and city-states. In this part of the world the *separate parts* always represented infinitely more than their *sum*. In German politics, pluralism with all its inherent discord – by definition something vague, inconstant, and threatening – has been a constant, one the rest of Europe has been quite happy to tolerate, in spite of all the risks it entailed. For when we attempted to find an answer to the German question by mustering a massive national order – first in 1871 and then more violently in 1933 – these shrill responses led sooner or later to catastrophe. Now there are only partial states left, co-existing within the context of co-existing power blocks, as the historian Theodor Schieder once put it. Beyond that, however, memories of something else have survived – a language, culture, landscape, a multitude of German characteristics in life and art – and a wish to preserve them from the undertow of the modern age, its practicality and cement, and its genuine or pretended economic necessities.

### II.

So much for today's "reality," as it has been shaped by the past. Yet even the most cynical materialist would probably admit that facts or political and economic power structures are not the only things that count. There is also a "Germany" that exists as an idea or image – one that has been invested with much that is noble and sublime, but also abused with such disastrous results – and it consists of more than romantic or chauvinistic phrases or the slogans that enabled politicians to lead and mislead. Nowadays, it is true, ambitious young executives or intellectuals are suspicious of such emotionally loaded words as "homeland" or "fatherland." They feel they have outgrown all that – and then tend to compensate by becoming all the more fanatic "patriots" of their local or national sports teams, in soccer matches or during the Olympics, for example. But these young people, who would like to think that they are "cured" of patriotism and that their native country is merely a sort of business address or practical affiliation, are often surprised to find their heritage catching up with them as they get older. They must confront the – sometimes

9

frightening – realization that their rejection of everything German contained a great deal of fear that it might touch them after all. No one can be German and remain completely unaffected by it, much as they might like to. We German survivors of the twentieth century have been indelibly stamped by a common language, history, culture, and experience of disaster. Hardly a single family escaped the dislocations and upheavals of the war. And hardly a single individual has become such a slave to the demands of reality that he does not sometimes have a vague inkling of Germany's indestructible essence. Someone who wants to perceive and catch hold of this other Germany, this hidden but by no means vanished place, would do well to leave home – and to return able to make comparisons. "People who never go abroad," I once wrote, "are too hard on their own country." I could have added: People who do not leave at some point and then return may not look at their own country with the necessary curiosity and passion. The famous photographer Michael Ruetz is German by birth – "a Hamburger from Berlin" – but he has worked abroad for a long time and spent many years in the United States, where he created his impressive volume of photographs entitled *Eye on America*. Now Ruetz has returned to Germany, to rediscover his homeland. As his pictures show, he saw things we often repress. He certainly did not come in order to criticize his old country, nor to expose deficiencies or document suffering. His fierce gaze often took in our postwar Germany as a work of art, a heightened Wagnerian world stage. Ruetz has a vision and dream of Germany as it "really" is: a canvas almost devoid of human figures, a composition of heroic landscape and clouds, with a lowering atmosphere. This is how at times we recall certain places of our childhood, where we realized for the first time how near, how overwhelming and mysterious, a castle, a forest, a house, a garden, or a beach could be.

## III.

Every traveler who prefers high speeds because he or she is eager to see as much as possible should be confronted with the paradoxical wisdom of hikers and cyclists: Nothing separates us from a landscape or a tourist attraction more than – glass! A car windshield or express-train window keep the surroundings at a distance. All the objects of our fleeting curiosity seem to lose their special aura – it must be so – when they rush past us behind glass, when we see them through an intervening layer. It seems possible that this inconspicuous glass, behind which modern tourists so like to take cover, is more of a hindrance to unclouded perception than even the most massive prejudice. In Julia Vosnessenkaya's book of interviews, *What Russians Think About Germans*, the author admits she was full of preconceptions to begin with: "What struck me about Germany was that it was so green.... The Soviet press had hammered it into us that there was no open country left in Germany, not a blade of grass, only industry. But my first impression was: God loves this land and its people, since they love their land. Wherever you looked, you saw something to make the heart rejoice." And the Russian writer Vladimir Voinovitch waxes enthusiastic: "Let me begin with the landscape. Germany is one of the most beautiful countries, and I think the explanation lies in its extremely mild and humid climate. The landscape is really very, very beautiful...."

The grandiose beauty of nature, as Wagner imagined it in *Tannhäuser*, in *Rheingold*, or *Siegfried*, also overwhelms us in the "two-eyed pictures" of Michael Ruetz, which combine sky and light, immediacy and the horizon into a *Gesamtkunstwerk* of photographic art. Roaming among them with your eyes open, you discover – virtually everywhere except for views of the sea – what affectionate nostalgia prompted him to seek out on his return home: trees....

Ruetz feels, he sees and desires that Germany can sense its own true nature only where trees still grow – regardless of whether he has his camera trained on mountain landscapes (like those painted by Caspar David Friedrich) or an industrial tract where a few trees have managed to survive (for the time being), or urban centers where foliage huddles at the foot of towering office buildings....

Claudel, the French Catholic writer whose feelings about Germany were truly ambivalent, once remarked, "Inside every real German there is both a mountain miner and a forester." Ruetz must have had this observation in mind when he saw and photographed Germany as a symphony of mountains and trees. In this way he caught something that typifies and stamps us as Germans to a greater extent than many Germans are aware, especially those who tend not to think about such things and who needed "acid rain" to remind them that trees "somehow" form part of our existence.

### IV.

What is so special about German forests? When we speak of them we rarely mean merely modern commercial forestry or the timber industry: There are overtones of the *Freischütz*; the words conjure up visions of the white hart and Varus' encounter with a terrible prophetess. Here sits Siegfried under the limewood tree thinking of his mother; while in another part of the forest Hansel and Gretel are losing their way and the witch Lorelei is taking the knight captive, as in Schumann's song: "Es ist schon spät, es ist schon kalt, kommst nimmermehr aus diesem Wald." ("It is late, it is cold, you will never get out of this forest alive.") Ancient Germanic pantheism, longings to escape from civilization, and a vital irrationality have all contributed their part to the mythology surrounding the German forest. (And "myth" here does not mean humbug or falsehood or delusion;

myths are ways of preserving patterns of experience, and the "truth" they contain is just as difficult to disprove as to prove.) The forest offers a refuge from human tyranny but also the possibility of escaping from the demands of democratic politics.

Germans who like to take walks through their woods might find Socrates lacking in imagination when he taught that he could "learn nothing from trees and streams." Many people today are still surprised by the way so many Germans can go into raptures over nature. Michael Ruetz has photographed Germany as if he shared this enthusiasm. Not everyone does. I well recall how a famous Jewish intellectual responded when asked if he didn't want to come for a walk in the woods: "We Jews don't go to the woods; we prefer to go to cafés." At the time I thought it was a joke, but in the meantime I have come to realize how much seriousness the remark probably contained, and how much intellectual passion for conversation and debate. The director Fritz Kortner, who was forced to leave the theatrical world in the old Berlin of the 1920s and flee to America (where he unavoidably had less of a reputation as an actor and artist, and where his view of art aroused less interest), lived in California. His old friend Elisabeth Neumann-Viertel, who had also emigrated to California, recounts a tragi-comic story about trying to take a walk. "We went for a walk with Kortner. At a point high above the ocean, where the view was breathtaking, Kortner gestured expansively at the whole panorama and said, 'I can't stand the sight of it.'"

### V.

Some of the landscapes in this volume seem to express without words, so to speak, the same idea as Arthur Schopenhauer in *The World as Will and Idea*:

*Let us imagine ourselves transported to a very lonely place, with an unlimited horizon, under a completely cloudless sky, trees and plants in the perfectly motionless air, no animals, no people, no running water, the deepest silence. Such surroundings are like a call to earnestness and contemplation, severing us from all our paltry desires: but this is just what gives to such surroundings which are merely lonely and deeply peaceful a touch of the sublime.*

How German! And how surprising to find Schopenhauer the skeptic expressing the mystical reflection that nature needs our gaze to be what it is. Ernst Bloch has noted how Schopenhauer's idea reappears in Wagner's *Parsifal*, where it is said of Nature: "She cannot see herself on the cross, and so she raises her eyes to redeemed humanity," *to the Easter light that shines behind Good Friday*, so that "Nature freed from sin achieves today its day of innocence." It is hard to imagine what a clever French writer, an Italian musician, or a British intellectual would think of such Germanic Schopenhauerian-Wagnerian speculations about Nature. Probably it would strike them as terribly deep and Teutonic…

## VI.

One can't help noticing that some of Ruetz's landscapes reproduce this German tendency toward Nature worship as if it were the most natural thing in the world. Yet it is hardly his intention to idealize or trivialize the towering German forests or the idyllic fields, valleys, villages, and towns in his photographs. In both nature and civilization as he has captured them, there is often more than a hint of threat, an archaic quality, those "ancient and neurotic foundations" mentioned by Thomas Mann in his speech on "Germany and the Germans." Such visions, such qualities, foundations, and backgrounds cannot be expressed in statistics, but neither can they simply be dismissed as irrational. We must try to live with them and gain control over them when they rise out of the mists of the past, in the visions of sharp-eyed artists, philosophers, commentators, and photographers.

Of course it is possible to ask whether all this "feeling for Nature" does not have a disturbingly antirational component. Perhaps our nation's relatively weak and only recently developed talent for democracy is connected with all of this, and our fatal irrationality that has made us such easy marks for dictators. "This is the Germans' greatest fault – that despite their intelligence and courage they always worship power," Winston Churchill once said, a man who was not exactly fussy about using power himself. And Nietzsche showed a keen sense for the connections between enthusiasm for nature, youthful immaturity, a sense of mystery, and "profundity" in the German soul when he wrote in *Beyond Good and Evil*:

*The German soul has passageways in it and passageways between the passageways; inside there are caves, hiding-places, dungeons, and this disorderliness has much of the charm of the mysterious. Germans are familiar with the secret paths that lead to chaos. And because every thing loves its own symbolic image, Germans love clouds and everything that is obscure, not yet fully formed, dimly lit, damp, and overcast: They feel that anything uncertain, shapeless, shifting, or growing in any way is "profound." Germans themselves are not in a state of "being" but rather of "becoming"; they are always "developing." "Development" is a truly German discovery, the German contribution to the great realm of philosophical ideas…*

## VII.

All the same it would be foolish to turn enthusiasm for nature, and love of one's homeland or forests into moral categories – to give them good or bad marks. A bit of relaxed wisdom would do no harm here, such as the cheerful insight contained in the Chinese writer Lin Yutang's question: "What is patriotism except love for the good things we had to eat when we were children?"... Of course it may also turn out that the German passion for trees, forests, and animate nature is a blessing, not just for us at the moment, but for the whole world! For this passion makes us more sensitively aware of what the murderous victory of technology over nature nowadays actually means. It is no wonder that the German political party of the "Greens" was the first to point out where all the enormously plausible "needs" of modern industry could lead.

In other countries people grinned a bit at first, taking these worries for the typically German hysteria of provincial alarmists. Their smiles began to fade, however, when the expression "Wald-sterben" ("dying forests") began to enter other languages, when oil spills threatened more than just the North Sea, and the hole in the ozone layer appeared in the sky as well as in the media. To put it another way: German enthusiasm for nature, which has often been criticized as sentimental and reactionary (and not without good cause), can actually prove to be a prophetic and progressive warning, if only the right conclusions are drawn and implemented.

This is a warning which political movers and shakers in West Germany ought to take seriously and include in their plans. The marvelously affirmative photographs of Michael Ruetz give us a vision of how much beauty, majesty, and hidden poetry are still to be found in our country, this postwar Germany. The developments threatening it all are encouraged not by "evil" manipulators, but by perfectly well-meaning experts, technicians, corporate managers, automobile manufacturers, and consumers. None of them wants a catastrophe; they just want to go on doing what seems to them sensible, feasible, and lucrative – without interference. Here Michael Ruetz's pictures, which attempt to envision and capture the soul of our landscape below the surface of Germany's workaday reality, can remind us of how much is at stake in the world-wide game of consumerism.

"I saw no phoenix rising out of Germany's ashes, but I did see a peacock," the poet Christoph Meckel once joked bitterly. But even a peacock needs clean air and decent food. Ernst Jünger does not lay all the blame at the feet of "industry" and the ruthless desire to make more money, when he laments the destruction of trees:

*Forests are disappearing, the old tree trunks are felled, and this is not to be explained by economics alone. Economics play a secondary role here, completing what was begun elsewhere, for we live in a time of incomparable wastefulness. This corresponds to its two greatest tendencies: standardization and acceleration. What is high must fall and age loses respect.*

Thus it is a consolation – and a warning – that trees still appear in almost all the photographs in this book. As Wolf Jobst Siedler has pointed out, modern dictators like to cut down trees. Their gigantic parade grounds – Red Square, Mussolini's Forum, Hitler's May Field, Peking's Tiananmen Square – all have no trees, for they would interfere with the parades, and make crowd control difficult. "To increase firing range it is always necessary to cut down trees."

Things have not gone quite that far yet at the places Michael Ruetz viewed through the affectionate eye of his camera. He had the artistic vision to discover a Germany that we can only hope will never be contradicted by reality.

# Plates

19 Weinheim on the Bergstrasse, Baden-Württemberg

A medieval town north of Heidelberg situated on the romantic route of the Bergstrasse and famous for its mild climate, its orchards, and its small towns.

20–21 Sigmaringen Castle, Baden-Württemberg

The castle, parts of which date from the twelfth century (the rest of it is a pastiche of all sorts of styles) was built on a rock rising out of the valley at the mouth of the upper Danube gap. During its long history it served as a camp of internment after World War II. The French author Louis Ferdinand Céline, under the accusation of being a collaborator with the Nazis, was imprisoned here.

22–23 The Rhine near Boppard, Rhineland-Palatinate

The Rhine, with its length of 820 miles, links four European countries, from the Alps to the North Sea. It has been a source not only of political controversies among its neighbors but also of legends that have formed around its castles, islands, and vineyards.

25–27 Field of stubble near Brunbyllund, Schleswig-Holstein

The wide northern plains between Hamburg and the Danish border, formerly poor moorland soil, have been made arable by modern drainage methods.

28–29 Holstein cattle near Olpenitzhof, Schleswig-Holstein

The marshy land near the Baltic coast is ideal pastureland for the breed of milk cattle that originated in this area.

30 Small village near Greding, Bavaria

The Franconian part of Bavaria north of Munich is unspoiled by tourism but offers all the charm of undulating fertile hills, small rural villages, and peaceful towns.

31 Cologne

Cologne is one of Germany's oldest and biggest cities. It was founded as early as 50 B.C. by the Romans, who named it Colonia Claudia Agrippinensis, after the wife of the Roman emperor Claudius. The spires of the Gothic cathedral, founded in 1248 and finished more than 600 years later, in 1880, rise to a height of 515 feet (157 meters) and form the most imposing part of Cologne's skyline as seen from the right bank of the Rhine.

32 Pfullingen, Baden-Württemberg

Pfullingen is a typical example of a whole chain of small industrial towns in the Swabian Jura, a range of limestone plateaux in the prosperous southwest of the country.

31

35    Comburg, Baden-Württemberg

Comburg, near Schwäbisch Hall, is one of the most impressive fortified abbeys in Germany. Huge walls and towers form an oval around the abbey church with its three Romanesque (twelfth century) towers and the enormous baroque hall, famous for the gilded chandelier from 1130.

36–37    Trarbach on the Moselle, Rhineland-Palatinate

The Moselle Valley between Trier and Koblenz is famous for its white wines. Due to the relatively northern situation of the area, the wines used to be so dry that winegrowers sometimes sweetened the juice rather heavily, a habit that, fortunately, viticulturists are giving up nowadays.

38–39    Haigerloch, Baden-Württemberg

This tiny town on the northern edge of the Swabian Jura has often been called the pearl of the Hohenzollerns. It is set between two rocks that were formerly crowned by medieval fortresses. Ruins of one of them are still to be seen above the narrow valley.

40    Siegmundshall potassium mine and cows
near Idensen, Lower Saxony

Germany's potassium industry is still important on the international market; before World War I the country produced 96 percent of the potassium in the world.

41    Bingsheim on the Rhine, Westphalia

The Rhine-Ruhr Basin, the greatest single industrial area in Europe, is undergoing a change now, but steelworks and coal mines are still a familiar sight in this vast man-made cityscape.

42–43    Water-meadow near Lichtenau, Spessart, Bavaria

Meandering rivers with unregulated courses have become a rare sight in this country.

44–45    Wooded ravine in the Allgäu, Bavaria

The western part of the Bavarian mountain region is the great cheese-manufacturing area of Germany.

46–47    Haystacks near Walmannshofen, Bavaria

49–51    Potassium mine "Siegfried," Giesen near Hannover, Lower Saxony

Mines of all kinds are often personalized by Christian names.

52    Schrecken-Manklitz, Allgäu, Bavaria

Pines are the most common trees in Bavaria now, allowing the fastest harvest. After an average life span of seventy years, a tree can be felled and used.

53    Ship on the Baltic Sea, near Kiel, Schleswig-Holstein

Since 1895 the Baltic and the North Sea have been linked by the Kiel Canal, the busiest in the world.

54–55    Beach chairs, Nordstrand, Schleswig-Holstein

Nordstrand belongs to an archipelago of small, flat islands scattered in the North Sea. The once hard and isolated life of the farmers and fishermen here has been radically changed by tourism – and in some cases by bridges – linking the islands with the mainland.

56    Schlei Island in the Baltic Sea, Schleswig-Holstein

The Baltic coast is so flat and, due to its lack of tides, calm, that land and sea make no sharp contrast.

59  Castle Stolzenfels, on the Rhine, Rhineland-Palatinate

Stolzenfels, south of Koblenz, is just one of a large number of castles on both sides of the famous Rhine Valley. It was reconstructed in the neo-Gothic style during the romance-loving nineteenth century; today it is a museum.

60–61  The Cathedral in Altenberg, Rhineland-Westphalia

Twenty kilometers (twelve and one-half miles) east of Cologne, in the hills of the Bergisches Land, this cathedral is a typical example of a fourteenth-century Cistercian abbey in pure Gothic style. Today, the abbey church is used for both Protestant and Catholic services.

62–63  Glücksburg Castle, Schleswig-Holstein

Erected in 1587 on the site of an abbey, Glücksburg is known as "the castle of happiness." A chef d'oeuvre of the renaissance in the north, it seems to float on the surrounding lake. The royal families of Denmark, Norway, and Greece are all in some way or another linked to this castle; Duke John the Younger of Schleswig-Holstein, who had the castle built, was their forefather.

64–65  Runkel, Lahn Valley, Hesse

The Lahn Valley is certainly the center of romantic Germany. Since the days of Johann Wolfgang von Goethe, it has been visited for its ruined castles and small towns. The thirteenth- to fifteenth-century castle here, guarding the bridge over the river, stands like a shield over the medieval village.

66  Beer garden, Reutberg Monastery in Upper Bavaria

Quiet beer gardens like this one near Bad Tölz are favorite spots for Sunday outings among families from Munich. Many monasteries still brew their own beer, which seems to taste best in the shade of a horse-chestnut tree.

67  Victory column, Berlin

The statue, commemorating Prussian wars of 1864, 1866, and 1870 overlooks Berlin's oldest public park.

68  Horse-chestnut tree in the Altmühl Valley, Bavaria

The Altmühl, a tributary of the Danube, flows through an until recently almost unspoiled valley famous for its varieties of rare wildflower and butterfly species. The construction of a navigable waterway connecting the Rhine, the Main, and the Danube, that is, Rotterdam with the Black Sea, will eventually put an end to this idyll.

69  House in Little Walser Valley, Austria

The secluded Little Walser Valley is a political curiosity due to its geographical situation. Cut off from Austria by the peaks of the Allgäu Alps, accessible only from Germany by a road that was built in 1930, the valley is under Austrian sovereignty, but economically it belongs to Germany; for example, the postage vans in the valley are German and the stamps issued here are Austrian.

70  Rothenburg on the Tauber, Bavaria

This town on the "Romantic Road" south of Würzburg still looks like the model of a German town in the Middle Ages. Its ramparts, paved streets, and old houses were the delight of nineteenth-century artists. Since then Rothenburg has been meticulously conserved for today's tourists, of which there are enormous crowds almost throughout the year. By sheer luck Rothenburg was spared World War II bombings; only the eastern part has had to be rebuilt.

73      Monschau, Eifel, Rhineland-Westphalia

Monschau, in the Eifel near Aachen, is famous for its slate roofs and half-timbered houses. High above the town towers the ruined castle of the Dukes of Montjois, who gave Monschau its name.

74      Wildenstein Castle on the Danube, Baden-Württemberg

The mainly sixteenth-century castle overlooks the Danube; it is fortified by two moats and two towers linked by a long wall.

75      Plane landing at the Frankfurt airport, Hesse

If Frankfurt on the Main is not Germany's capital, it certainly looks like it, with its mixture of old buildings and skyscrapers, its central situation, big railway station, and busy airport.

76–79      Völklingen on the Saar

Like the Ruhr Basin, the Saar Valley near the French border is dominated by heavy industry, in this case, steelworks. Like the Ruhr, the Saar area needs a change; German steelworks are mostly unprofitable today due to the price competition on the world market, so the Ruhr and the Saar suffer from high unemployment rates.

80      Power station in Frimmersdorf, Rhineland-Westphalia

Huge beds of lignite, or brown coal, are mined west of Cologne. The surface-mining process destroys large parts of the landscape. The area here is seen as a model case: all exploited mines are recultivated immediately after the ore is extracted.

81      The Brandenburg Gate, Berlin

The Brandenburg Gate, built in 1789, crowned by the famous four-in-hand of 1793, became the symbol of the divided city: it stands in the eastern sector, but is visible from the west.

82      Fasanerie (Pheasant Castle) in Fulda, Hesse

Fulda, founded as a Benedictine abbey in 744, still bears the signs of the power and worldly wealth of its Christian rulers. The baroque castle, completed by a prince-bishop in 1756, adds to the overall impression of baroque splendor.

83      The Berlin Wall

A detail of the "anti-imperialist wall of protection" that the East German government found it necessary to erect in August 1961. The wall, as seen here, consisted of a system of fences, a well-raked strip of soil (to make footprints visible), watchtowers, floodlights, and concrete.

84–85      Berlin

The detail from the previous page in an overall view.

87–89      Berlin

The aerial view from west to east shows the separation of Germany's former capital. The television tower stands on the Alexanderplatz, the showpiece of modern East Berlin. The hole in the wall is checkpoint Heinrich Heine Strasse, one of the passageways through the nowadays threadbare iron curtain.

90–91      Ediger on the Moselle

German wine growing is certainly not easy. The vineyards are steep and small, the climate much rougher than in the sunny parts of France and Italy.

92–93      Schwäbisch Hall, Baden-Württemberg

Salt springs gave this old town its wealth. It is built in tiers up the steep flanks of the Kocher valley; Schwäbisch Hall's market square is one of the most beautiful in the country.

94      The Pfalz, Kaub, Rhineland-Palatinate

The Pfalzgrafenstein, a castle used as a tollhouse from the twelfth to the nineteenth centuries, was erected on a rock in the Rhine.

95      Berlin

Typical of Berlin's nineteenth-century blocks of flats, there are several inner courtyards within the blocks, shaded by chestnut trees.

96      Röchling Saar Steelworks in Völklingen

A frequent sight in the industrial areas of the country: workers still live in the immediate neighborhood of the factories, counteracting the opressiveness of steelworks and coal mines by meticulously kept small gardens.

94

99         **Near Hohenstaufen, Baden-Württemberg**

Fields in the southwest of the country are often small. The tradition here is that a farmer bequeaths his farm to all his sons; consequently, the farms have been split into sometimes tiny units.

100–101     **Weltenburg Abbey on the Danube, Bavaria**

The river bend west of Regensburg offers a striking site for this small baroque abbey. It was built from 1714 to 1725, partly by the famous Asam brothers, architects and stucco artists.

102–103     **Mount Wendelstein, Bavaria**

At 6,030 feet (1,838 meters), the Wendelstein summit is a popular viewpoint in the Bavarian Alps. The top of the mountain holds not only the eighteenth-century chapel but also a transmitter station of Bavarian television.

104–105     **The Zugspitze, Bavaria**

This is the highest peak of the German Alps (9,730 feet or 2,966 meters) accessible from Austria by cable car, from Bavaria by an underground train. On clear days the panorama is stunning, allowing views of the Austrian and Swiss Alps and the Bavarian lowland with its lakes.

106–107     **Moonrise in the Black Forest, Baden-Württemberg**

The Black Forest, a mountain region in the southwest, separated from the French Vosges by the Rhine Valley, is a popular resort for both walking and skiing.

108–109     **Schrecken-Manklitz, Allgäu, Bavaria**

The Allgäu, much visited for its royal castles, Linderhof and Neuschwanstein, is less spectacular but certainly charming in the peaceful rural area north of the Alps.

110       **Hatzenport on the Moselle, Rhineland-Palatinate**

More and more vineyards on the Rhine and Moselle are being given up; behind the church, typical of the area with its white-and-red paint, overgrown terraces are to be seen next to cultivated ones.

113 **Worpswede, Lower Saxony**

This village, in the peat bogland near Bremen, came to fame as an artists' colony at the turn of the century, when painters like Mackensen, Modersohn, Overbeck, and Paula Modersohn-Becker settled here to work.

114 **Sunset over Goslar, Lower Saxony**

The key to Goslar's importance is the silver and lead mines that have been worked since the Middle Ages. The Salian emperors (1024–1125) made Goslar their residence; around 1500 the prosperity of the city grew with the wealth of its burghers, whose timber-fronted houses and town hall are still to be seen today.

115 **Völklingen on the Saar**

The glow of liquid steel looks like a man-made sunset.

116–117 **Weissach-Valley near Oberstaufen in the Allgäu, Bavaria**

This area northeast of Lake Constance, near the Swiss and Austrian borders, abounds in popular holiday resorts.

118 **Weissweiler Power Station, Rhineland-Westphalia**

Typical for the Rhine-Ruhr area is this mixture of village idylls and monumental industrial complexes.

119 **Sigmaringen Castle, Baden-Württemberg**

A detailed description of this castle (see also pages 20–21) is to be found in the memoirs of the French author Louis Ferdinand Céline.

120 **Reichsburg Castle, Cochem, Rhineland-Palatinate**

Like many others in the area, this castle in the Moselle valley is a nineteenth-century reconstruction in fourteenth-century style. Today it houses a museum.

121 **Frankfurt on the Main**

Ever since the days of the Bethmanns and Rothschilds (1744–1912) Frankfurt has been Germany's banking capital; the modern bank buildings give the city its skyline.

122–123 **Schwäbische Alb near Teck, Baden-Württemberg**

The pastoral hills of the Swabian Jura southwest of Stuttgart afford views like this one, over small industrial tows typical of Germany's prosperous southwest.

124 **Siegfried potassium mine, in the Leine Valley, Lower Saxony**

The hills of white material (see also pages 49–51) are visible from long distances in the flat area around Hannover.

125 **In the Leine Valley, near Hannover, Lower Saxony**

Seemingly endless tree-lined roads, "chausseen" are a typical feature of the northeast.

126–127 **Bamberg, Bavaria**

It was the emperor Heinrich II (his coat, symbolizing sovereignty over the whole world, is still to be seen in Bamberg museum), who made the then called Babenberg into an episcopal town in 1007 and dreamed of a second Rome to be erected on its seven hills. For 800 years Bamberg, undestroyed by war, remained under the sovereignty of its prince-bishops. The episcopal quarter was situated in the upper town; the burgers lived in the valley. A centerpiece of the town's numerous works of art is the cathedral, founded in 1012, containing the famous equestrian statue of the Knight of Bamberg, an idealized thirteenth-century representation of a knight-king.

128 **Near Amöneburg, Kirchhain, Hesse**

This peaceful picture is not typical of any particular part of the country but rather of the whole. Such invariably neat kitchen gardens could also be found sqeezed in between factories or houses.

129 **Breitnau in the Black Forest, Baden-Württemberg**

A typical Black Forest house: the huge slate-covered roof that contains the barn is steep so that the heavy winter snow cannot build up and put too much weight on it. The house itself is insulated by small wooden tiles made of local material; the long balconies under the roof can be used for drying washing and crops.

130–131　Neuenstein Castle, near Schwäbisch Hall,
Baden-Württemberg

The sixteenth-century residence of the dukes of Hohenlohe in the middle of the rural Hohenlohe plain between Stuttgart and Würzburg still gives a good impression of daily life in a small German court.

132–133　Beech forest in the Süsing, Lüneburg Heath,
Lower Saxony

In the Middle Ages, the heart of Europe was covered with almost impenetrable woods, areas the traveler had to fear; the nineteenth-century romantic movement discovered what was left of them as walking areas for city dwellers.

134–135　Hofoldinger Forest, Bavaria

Whereas the beech forests are typical of the north, pine plantations are to be found mainly in the south, where they have replaced the original mixed woods.

136–137　Lake Hintersee, Ramsau, near Berchtesgaden,
Bavaria

This lake, much less well known and overcrowded than the famous Königssee is popular among walkers who like to escape from the summer crowds.

139–141　The Rhine near Kaub, Rhineland-Palatinate

The foldout page shows the overall view of the detail on page 94: the Rheinpfalz, the old tollcastle on its rock in the river, is overlooked by the restored ruins of Castle Gutenfels.

142–143　Limburg on the Lahn Valley, Hesse

The cathedral, built between 1210 and 1250, overlooking the Lahn Valley from its rock, is a good example of Gothic transitional style.

144–145　Monreal in the Eltz Valley, Rhineland-Palatinate

Half-timbered houses are a feature of many small towns in the Eifel plateau west of the Rhine Valley.
The Eltz is a small westen tributary of the Moselle, which it joins at the famous Eltz castle, a picture of which is to be seen on the 500 DM banknote.

146–147　Homberg, Efze, Hesse

The stadtkirche (main church) in the center of this town is a kind of memorial to Protestantism, which was introduced into Hesse in this church in 1526. The building is Gothic, parts of it dating from 1374.

Bremisch-Hannoversche
Eisenbahn AG

140

BOE

118

124

126

# Postscript

What is the hardest thing of all?
What seems the easiest:
For your eyes to see
What lies before them.

Johann Wolfgang von Goethe
and Friedrich Schiller, *Xenien*

Before the invention of photography, travelers preserved their impressions of what they saw in sketchbooks: The traveler made sketches whereas the tourist now takes snapshots. The process of making pictures to take home with one demanded such intense concentration on the subject that there was opportunity to practice self-criticism. Goethe, whose talents did not lie in the direction of drawing, realized "what sensitivity, what talent and practice are necessary to grasp the depth and breadth of a landscape as a picture!" (*Truth and Poetry*, Book 6).

The technical advance of photography has not altered that. A landscape is still an infinite space, and the elements of its composition are beyond reach. In order to make an expressive composition out of it, to "grasp it as a picture," the photographer must be able to predict how the pictorial elements present in three dimensions will relate to one another in two dimensions.

It makes no difference whether the representation of the landscape is to be a drawing or a photograph; paper and pen or lens and film are only technical aids and no substitute for ability.

In his struggles to draw, Goethe shifted his attention to other subjects: "to enclosed spaces, where I achieved some results." With his limited talents he had more success where the elements of the composition were close at hand. An enclosed space is easier to master.

Or to put it another way: A narrow view provides a sense of security. It excludes a number of arguments and makes one's own seem well-founded.

Landscapes, as views of wide-open spaces, usually don't fit in the picture. People prefer (because it is easier) to photograph a particular quarter of a city, small groups, even corridors. In this way one's own navel becomes more important than infinity.

In Germany, since the movement began against the kind of representational art that used to be required at art schools, photography – especially landscape photography – has acquired a bad reputation: It cannot provide the social criticism now demanded of artists and is even seen as distracting our attention from more important matters. Many people think that interest in "the depth and breadth of a landscape" automatically implies bad taste, and they mean not only pictures of it but the thing itself.

This is a mistaken attitude, which sees everything beautiful as tasteless and recognizes only what is ugly as true. The art of photography, the art of what is outwardy visible, cannot be concerned with the political fashions of the moment. Its task is one which never gets easier: to see what is before our eyes.

Germany is Germany wherever you go, not only in the places where you can "do the sights," where its castles are "enshrined in legend," its forests "deep," the region is "idyllic," the landscape "photogenic," where the half-timbered houses are "romantic," the valleys "peaceful," the panoramas "charming," the villages "picturesque," and their inhabitants "typical." I have never met a "typical German," nor have I ever noticed anyone at work enshrining castles in legend. Unfortunately the forests are no longer as deep as I would like; the valleys usually have a highway running through them; the panoramas tend to be boring, and I don't have much desire to live in a village of half-timbered houses. I just love to look at them. But Germany is, after all, also the country where the suburbs and new buildings are supposed to be "faceless" (although what about the people who live there? And isn't this precisely what typifies our cities for us?) and the countryside is supposedly "overbuilt." Yet all of this is worth seeing – to us. And why should we care about tourists? Why can't we just be ourselves?

The automatic epithets make thinking superfluous and thus make us and our own reactions superfluous: We don't need to look anymore.

No doubt about it, Germany is a beautiful country. What that means is something everyone can define for himself or herself. I could imagine that the real beauty of Germany, which lies for me personally in the realm of the unspectacular, is not evident to anyone who hasn't lived here for a long time. Nowhere else is the progression of the seasons so clear: four times a year the country changes. The area around Ayers Rock in Australia, on the other hand, is always the same. Nowhere else does there exist such a harmonious mixture of cultivated land and buildings as in the Chiemgau or the tributary valleys of the River Lahn. This is barely recognizable from outside or far away. The beauty of Germany eludes advertising. (Maybe it even eluded me.) You can find it only between the lines in bold type if you are reading a guidebook, where none of the major "attractions" interest me. Of course Castle Neuschwanstein, that wonderful absurdity, is part of Germany, but it belongs mostly to tourists and is almost foreign territory. What I love about this country is hamlets such as Anger or the beer garden in Reutberg, especially when I have them to myself. No bus comes to disgorge its passengers; the tourist brochures make no mention of them. They are beautiful without being spectacular, a last refuge. With every picture in this book I want to offer a paradigm for the whole of Germany – a study of the country in picture form, showing what the travel guides and "mood studies" fail to capture. Whether the result says more about me or the subject I leave for others to decide. My view of Germany, as it is to be seen here, is not intended for someone who plans to "do" the country in a couple of days.

These pictures are for us.

*Michael Ruetz*
*Munich, January 1990*

*Acknowledgments*
I am especially grateful to my wife for sharing the lengthy preparations for this book.

I am also indebted to Lufthansa, and in particular to Ruth von Schnakenburg of the Lufthansa Public Relations Department for her help in bringing this project to realization.

My sincere thanks go to the 7th Flight AAC Berlin-Gatow for expert guidance and wonderful hours over Berlin.

# List of Plates

2–3    Avenue of trees in Sieseby on the Schlei, Schleswig-Holstein

19    Weinheim on the Bergstrasse, Baden-Württemberg

20–21    Sigmaringen Castle, Baden-Württemberg

22–23    The Rhine near Boppard, Rhineland-Palatinate

25–27    Field of stubble near Brunbyllund, Schleswig-Holstein

28–29    Holstein cattle near Olpenitzhof, Schleswig-Holstein

30    Small village near Greding, Bavaria

31    Cologne

32    Pfullingen, Baden-Württemberg

35    Comburg, Baden-Württemberg

36–37    Trarbach on the Moselle, Rhineland-Palatinate

38–39    Haigerloch, Baden-Württemberg

40    Siegmundshall potassium mine and cows near Idensen, Lower Saxony

41    Bingsheim on the Rhine, Westphalia

42–43    Water-meadow near Lichtenau, Spessart, Bavaria

44–45    Wooded ravine in the Allgäu, Bavaria

46–47    Haystacks near Walmannshofen, Bavaria

49–51    Potassium mine "Siegfried," Giesen near Hannover, Lower Saxony

52    Schrecken-Manklitz in the Allgäu, Bavaria

53    Ship on the Baltic Sea near Kiel, Schleswig-Holstein

54–55    Beach chairs in Nordstrand, Schleswig-Holstein

56    Schlei Island in the Baltic Sea, Schleswig-Holstein

59    Castle Stolzenfels on the Rhine, Rhineland-Palatinate

60–61    The cathedral in Altenberg, Rhineland-Westphalia

62–63    Glücksburg Castle, Schleswig-Holstein

64–65    Runkel Lahn Valley, Hesse

66    Beer garden, Reutberg Monastery in Upper Bavaria

67    Victory column, Berlin

68    Horse-chestnut tree in the Altmühl Valley, Bavaria

69    House in Little Walser Valley, Austria

70    Rothenburg on the Tauber, Bavaria

73    Monschau, Eifel, Rhineland-Westphalia

74    Wildenstein Castle on the Danube, Baden-Württemberg

75    Plane landing at the Frankfurt airport, Hesse

77–79    Völklingen on the Saar

80    Power station in Frimmersdorf, Rhineland-Westphalia

81    The Brandenburg Gate, Berlin

82    Fasanerie (Pheasant Castle) in Fulda, Hesse

83    The Berlin Wall

84–85    Berlin

87–89    Berlin

90–91    Ediger on the Moselle

92–93    Schwäbisch Hall, Baden-Württemberg

94    The Pfalz, Kaub, Rhineland-Palatinate

95    Berlin

96    Röchling Saar Steelworks in Völklingen

99    Near Hohenstaufen, Baden-Württemberg

100–101    Weltenburg Abbey on the Danube, Bavaria

102–103    Mount Wendelstein, Bavaria

104–105    The Zugspitze, Bavaria

106–107    Moonrise in the Black Forest, Baden-Württemberg

108–109    Schrecken-Manklitz in the Allgäu, Bavaria

110    Hatzenport on the Moselle, Rhineland-Palatinate

113    Worpswede, Lower Saxony

114    Sunset over Goslar, Lower Saxony

115    Völklingen on the Saar

116–117    The Weissach Valley near Oberstaufen in the Allgäu, Bavaria

118    The Weissweiler Power Station, Rhineland-Westphalia

119    Sigmaringen Castle, Baden-Württemberg

120    Reichsburg Castle, Cochem, Rhineland-Palatinate

121    Frankfurt on the Main

122–123    The Schwäbische Alb near Teck, Baden-Württemberg

124    Siegfried potassium mine in the Leine Valley, Lower Saxony

125    In the Leine Valley, near Hannover, Lower Saxony

126–127    Bamberg, Bavaria

128        Near Amöneberg, Kirchhain,
           Hesse

129        Breitnau in the Black Forest,
           Baden-Württemberg

130–131    Neuenstein Castle near
           Schwäbisch Hall,
           Baden-Württemberg

132–133    Beech forest in the Süsing,
           Lüneburg Heath,
           Lower Saxony

134–135    Hofoldinger Forest, Bavaria

136–137    Lake Hintersee, Ramsau, near
           Berchtesgaden, Bavaria

139–141    The Rhine near Kaub,
           Rhineland-Palatinate

142–143    Limburg on the Lahn, Hesse

144–145    Monreal in the Eltz Valley,
           Rhineland-Palatinate

146–147    Homberg, Efze, Hesse

All the aerial photographs of Berlin are
released by permission of the Federal Air
Traffic Authority in Hamburg under the
number 402/89.